Why Christmas?

Nicky Gumbel

The Christmas edition of *Why Jesus?*

Illustrated by
Charlie
Mackesy

Why Christmas?

Why Christmas? (Expanded Edition)
© 2008 by Alpha International

Published in Nashville, Tennessee, by W Publishing Group, an imprint of Thomas Nelson. W Publishing Group and Thomas Nelson are registered trademarks of HarperCollins Christian Publishing, Inc.

Originally published by Kingsway Communications Ltd, Lottbridge Drove, Eastbourne, BN23 6NT, England. First printed by Alpha North America in 2001.

Any Internet addresses (websites, blogs, etc.) and telephone numbers in this book are offered as a resource. They are not intended in any way to be or imply an endorsement by Thomas Nelson, nor does Thomas Nelson vouch for the content of these sites and numbers for the life of this book.

All Scripture quotations, unless otherwise noted, are taken from The Holy Bible, New International Version® Anglicized, NIV®. Copyright © 1979, 1984, 2011 by Biblica, Inc.® Used by permission. All rights reserved worldwide.

Scripture quotations marked AMP taken from The Amplified Bible©. AMP©. Copyright © 2015 by The Lockman Foundation, La Habra, California 90631. Used by permission. All rights reserved.

Scripture quotations marked MSG taken from The Message©. MSG©. Copyright © 1993, 1994, 1995, 1996, 2000, 2001, 2002 by Eugene H. Peterson.

Illustrations by Charlie Mackesy

ISBN 978-1-938-3-2892-3

First Printing 2017 / Printed in the United States of America

Why Celebrate Christmas?

There is something almost magical about Christmas: children dream of Santa Claus and his fantasy sleigh, we picture Christmas trees, snowy scenes, filled-up stockings, piles of presents, and smiling families around the fire.

The reality is often not as perfect as we imagine. Some people go over the top at Christmas. The overcrowding on the streets and in the shops can lead to so-called "Santa-Claustrophobia."

Over-indulging takes its toll on family life. One nine-year-old boy wrote, "I know Christmas should be a religious time, but to me Christmas is a time for the necessities of life such as food, presents, and booze." Another boy wrote, "After breakfast we go into the sitting room. Dad comes in drunk with Mom's tights and an Indian hat on!" His teacher wrote in the margin, "Good old Dad!"

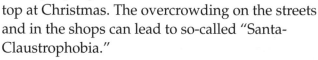

For some there is a danger of overspending—buying presents that others do not need with money they do not have.

One little girl wrote to her grandmother, "Thank you very much for the nice gloves you sent me for Christmas. They were something I wanted—but not very much!"

Others can become over-demanding. One doting father asked his small daughter well in advance what she would like for Christmas. Shyly she announced she would like a baby brother. To everyone's surprise and delight her mother returned from the hospital on Christmas Eve with a baby boy in her arms. When the father repeated the question next year, there was less hesitation. "If it wouldn't be too uncomfortable for Mommy, I would like a pony!"

But while some go over the top, others go under. For many, Christmas is one of the worst times of the year. Suicide rates go up, more people die from "natural causes," marriages fall apart, psychiatrists' patients suffer regressions, and family feuds begin.

One Mori poll suggested that there are three million family arguments each Christmas. A newspaper article headlined, "Enough to Drive You Crackers," spoke of people cracking up at Christmas as a result of the pressure to be perfect. It reported that two psychologists, a psychotherapist, and a counselor were running a workshop entitled "Stress in the Family: Coping with Christmas."  They said that part of its success seemed to be the chance it offered to get away from it all. The psychiatrist Anthony Storr in an article on depression at Christmas entitled, "Cheer Up, It's Soon Over," had this final piece of advice: "Remember that Christmas, although recurrent, doesn't last forever."

With all the magic, the stress, and the hype of Christmas, are we missing the point? What is at the heart of Christmas? In the words of C. S. Lewis, at Christmas we remember the "central event in the history of the earth—the very thing the whole story has been about."

WHY BOTHER WITH JESUS?

When Jesus was born, a group of highly intelligent philosophers thought He was worth bothering with. They stopped everything to take Him three symbolic presents. The first was gold—a present fit for a king. The child in the manger was the King of kings and Lord of lords. God Himself had come to live as part of our world.

Too often Jesus has been obscured by Christmas. One man wrote to The Times:

"Sir: Failing to find any religious books in the bookshop, I asked an assistant for help. She showed me an inconspicuous handful of Bibles and prayer books, saying: 'We have had to move them down to the bottom shelf because of Christmas.'"

But the point of Christmas is Jesus Christ. At Christmas we celebrate the birthday of the most important Person who has ever lived. He is the centerpiece of our civilization. After all, we call what happened before His birth B.C. and what happened after A.D.!

But how do we know it's true?

We can test the claims of Christianity because it is a historical faith. It is based on the life, death, and resurrection of Jesus Christ. Our faith is based on firm historical evidence.

Who is Jesus?

Jesus was and is the Son of God. Some people think He is just a "good religious teacher." However, that suggestion does not fit with the facts.

a) His claims

Jesus claimed to be the unique Son of God on an equal footing with God. He assumed the authority to forgive sins. He said that one day He would judge the world, and that what would matter then would be how we had responded to Him in this life.

C. S. Lewis pointed out, "A man who was merely a man and said the sort of things Jesus said wouldn't be a great moral teacher." He would either be insane or else He would be "the Devil of Hell." "You must make your choice," he writes. Either Jesus was, and is, the Son of God, or else He was insane or evil but, C. S. Lewis goes on, "let us not come up with any patronizing nonsense about Him being a great human teacher. He has not left that open to us. He did not intend to."

b) His character

Many people who do not profess to be Christians regard Jesus as the supreme example of a selfless life.

The Russian author Fyodor Dostoevsky, himself a Christian, said, "I believe there is no one lovelier, deeper, more sympathetic, and more perfect than Jesus. I say to myself, with jealous love, that not only is there no one else like him but there could never be anyone like him."

As far as Jesus' teaching is concerned, there seems to be a general agreement that it is the purest and best ever to have fallen from the lips of man.

As C. S. Lewis put it, "It seems obvious that he was neither a lunatic nor fiend; and consequently, however strange or terrifying or unlikely it may seem, I have to accept the view that he was and is God. God has landed on this enemy-occupied world in human form."

c) His conquest of death

The evidence for the physical resurrection is very strong indeed. When the disciples went to the tomb, they found the grave clothes had collapsed and Jesus' body was gone.

In the next six weeks He was seen by over 500 people. The disciples' lives were transformed, and the Christian church was born and grew at a dynamic rate.

A former Lord Chief Justice of England, Lord Darling, said of the resurrection: "In its favor as living truth there exists such overwhelming evidence, positive and negative, factual and circumstantial, that no intelligent jury in the world could fail to bring in a verdict that the Resurrection story is true." The only satisfactory explanation for these facts is that Jesus did indeed rise from the dead and thus confirm that He was, and is, the Son of God.

The wise men were right. Nothing less than gold would be suitable for such a child.

Why Do We Need Jesus?

Even if Jesus was who He said He was, why do we need Him 2,000 years later? The second gift the wise men brought was frankincense, which was used in the temple as the symbol of prayer, and pointed to a relationship with God.

Relationships are exciting! They are the most important aspect of our lives—our relationships with our parents, boyfriend or girlfriend, husband or wife, children, grandchildren, friends, coworkers, and so on.

Christianity is first and foremost about relationships rather than rules. It's about a Person more than a philosophy. It is about the most important relationship of all—our relationship with the God who made us. Jesus said that the first and greatest commandment is to love God. The second is to love our neighbor. So it is also about our relationships with other people.

You and I were created to live in a relationship with God. Until we find that relationship there will always be something missing in our lives. As a result, we are often aware of a gap. One rock singer described it by saying: "I've got an emptiness deep inside."

A woman, in a letter to me, wrote of "a deep, deep void." Another young girl spoke of a "chunk missing in her soul."

People try to fill this emptiness in various ways. Some try to close the gap with money—but that does not satisfy. Aristotle Onassis, who was one of the richest men in the world, said at the end of his life, "Millions do not always add up to what a man needs out of life."

Others try drugs or alcohol abuse or sexual promiscuity. One girl said, "These things provide instant gratification, but they leave you feeling hollow afterwards." Still others try hard work, music, or sports, while others seek success. There may not be anything wrong with these in themselves, but they do not satisfy that hunger deep inside every human being.

Even the closest human relationships, wonderful though they are, do not in themselves satisfy this "emptiness deep inside." Nothing will fill this gap except the relationship with God for

14

which we were made.

According to the New Testament, the reason for this emptiness is that men and women have turned their backs on God.

Jesus said, "I am the bread of life" (John 6:35). He is the only one who can satisfy our deepest hunger because He is the one who makes it possible for us to be restored to a relationship with God.

a) He satisfies our hunger for meaning and purpose in life

At some point everyone asks the question, "What am I doing on Earth?" or "What is the point of life?" or "Is there any purpose in life?" As the philosopher and author Albert Camus once said, "Man cannot live without meaning."

Until we are living in relationship with God we will never find the true meaning and purpose of life. Other things may provide passing satisfaction, but it does not last. Only in a relationship with our Creator do we find the true meaning and purpose of our lives.

b) He satisfies our hunger for life beyond death

Before I was a Christian I did not like to think

about the subject of death. My own death seemed a long way in the future. I didn't know what would happen and I didn't want to think about it. I was failing to face up to reality. The fact is that we will all die. Yet the Bible says, "He has also set eternity in the hearts of men" (Ecclesiastes 3:11). Most people don't want to die. We long to survive beyond death. Only in Jesus Christ do we find eternal life, for our relationship with God, which starts now, survives death and goes on into eternity.

c) He satisfies our hunger for forgiveness

If we are honest, we would have to admit that we all do things that we know are wrong. Sometimes we do things for which we are deeply ashamed. More than that, there is a self-centeredness about our lives which spoils them. Jesus said, "What comes out of a man is what makes him 'unclean.' For from within, out of men's hearts, come evil thoughts, sexual immorality, theft, murder, adultery, greed, malice, deceit, lewdness, envy, slander, arrogance and folly. All these evils come from inside and make a man 'unclean.'" (Mark 7:20-23).

Our greatest need is for forgiveness. Just as a man who has cancer needs a doctor whether he realizes it or not, so we need forgiveness whether we realize it or not. Just as with cancer, the man who recognizes his need is far better off than the person who is lulled into a false sense of security.

By His death on the cross Jesus made it possible for us to be forgiven and brought back into a relationship with God. At Christmas we remember the fact that Jesus entered our world in order to restore relationships—first our relationship with God and then our relationships with others. In this way, He supplied the answer to our deepest need.

Why Did He Come To Earth?

Why did Jesus come? How would He achieve this restoration of our relationship with God? The third present the wise men brought gives us the answer. Myrrh was used to embalm the bodies of the dead.

Jesus is the only man who has ever chosen to be born, and He is one of the few who has chosen to die. He said that the entire reason for His coming was to die for us. "The Son of Man [came] . . . to give his life as a ransom for many" (Mark 10:45). The supreme reason for giving Christmas presents is to remind us of His gift to us—the most valuable and expensive gift ever given.

From what we know of crucifixion, it was one of the cruelest forms of death known to man. Cicero, a first-century Roman statesman, described it as "the most cruel and hideous of tortures." Jesus would have been flogged with a whip of several strands of leather weighted with pieces of metal and bone. According to Eusebius, a third-century historian, "The sufferer's veins were laid bare, and the very muscles, sinews, and bowels of the victim were opened to exposure." Jesus was then forced to carry a six-foot beam until He collapsed. When He reached the site of execution, His hands and feet were nailed to the cross with six-inch nails. He was left to hang for hours of excruciating pain.

Yet the New Testament makes it clear that there was something worse for Jesus than the physical and emotional pain—that was the spiritual anguish of being separated from God as He carried all our sins.

Why did He die?

Jesus said He died for us. The word "for" means "instead of." He did it because He loves us and did not want us to have to pay the penalty for all the things that we have done wrong. On the cross, He was effectively saying, "I will take all those wrong things on myself."

He did it for you and He did it for me. If you or I had been the only person in the world, He would have done it for us. The apostle Paul wrote of "the Son of God, who loved me and gave himself for me" (Gal. 2:20). It was out of love for us that He gave His life as a ransom.

The word "ransom" comes from the slave market. A kind man might buy a slave and set him or her free—but first he had to pay the ransom price. Jesus paid, by His blood on the cross, the ransom price to set us free.

Freedom from what?

a) Freedom from guilt

Whether we feel guilty or not, we are all guilty before God because of the many times we have broken His laws in thought, word, or deed. Just as when someone commits a crime there is a penalty to be paid, so there is a penalty for breaking God's spiritual laws. "The wages of sin is death" (Romans 6:23). The result of the things we do wrong is spiritual death—being cut off from God forever. We all deserve to suffer that penalty. On the cross, Jesus took the penalty in our place so we could be totally forgiven and our guilt could be taken away.

b) Freedom from addiction

The things that we do wrong are like an addiction. Jesus said, "Everyone who sins is a slave to sin" (John 8:34). Jesus died to set us free from that slavery. On the cross, the power of this addiction was broken. Although we may still fall from time to time, the power of this addiction is broken when Jesus sets us free. That is why Jesus went on to say, "If the Son sets you free, you will be free indeed" (John 8:36).

c) Freedom from fear

Jesus came "so that by his death he might destroy him who holds the power of death—that is, the devil—and free those who all their lives were held in slavery by their fear of death" (Hebrews 2:14-15). We need no longer fear death.

Death is not the end for those whom Jesus has set free. Rather, it is the gateway to heaven, where we will be free from even the presence of sin. When Jesus set us free from the fear of death, He also set us free from all other fears.

Freedom for what?

Jesus is no longer physically on earth, but He has not left us alone. He has sent His Holy Spirit to be with us. When His Spirit comes to live within us, He gives us a new freedom.

a) Freedom to know God

The things that we do wrong cause a barrier between us and God—"Your iniquities have separated you from your God" (Isaiah 59:2).

When Jesus died on the cross, He removed the barrier that was between us and God. As a result, He has made it possible for us to have a relationship with our Creator. We become His sons and daughters. The Spirit assures us of this relationship, and He helps us to get to know God better. He helps us to pray and to understand God's Word (the Bible).

b) Freedom to love

"We love because he first loved us" (I John 4:19). As we look at the Cross we understand God's love for us. When the Spirit of God comes to live within us, we experience that love. As we do so we receive a new love for God and for other people. We are set free to live a life of love—to live a life centered around loving and serving Jesus and loving and serving other people, rather than a life centered around ourselves.

c) Freedom to change

People sometimes say, "You are what you are. You can't change." The good news is that with the help of the Spirit we can change. The Holy Spirit gives us the freedom to live the sort of lives that, deep down, we have always wanted to live. The apostle Paul tells us that the fruit of the Spirit is "love, joy, peace, patience, kindness, goodness, faithfulness, gentleness, and self-control" (Galatians 5:22, 23a). When we ask the Spirit of God to come and live within us, these wonderful characteristics begin to grow in our lives.

Why Not?

So, God offers us forgiveness and freedom in Christ Jesus and His Spirit to live within us. All this is a gift from God. When someone offers us a present, we have a choice. We can accept it, open it, and enjoy it, or we can refuse the gift and say, "No, thank you." Sadly, many people make excuses for not accepting the gift God offers.

Here are some of the excuses:

a) "I have no need of God"

When people say this, they usually mean they are quite happy without God. What they fail to realize is that our greatest need is not "happiness" but "forgiveness." It takes a very proud person to say he or she has no need of forgiveness.

We all need to be forgiven. Without forgiveness we are in serious trouble. For God is not only our loving Father, He is also a righteous judge.

Either we accept what Jesus has done for us on the cross, or else one day we will pay the just penalty ourselves for the things we have done wrong.

b) "There is too much to give up"

Sometimes, God puts His finger on something in our lives that we know is wrong and that we need to give up if we want to enjoy this relationship with God through Jesus.

But we need to remember:

- God loves us. He only asks us to give up things that do us harm. If my children were playing with a carving knife I would tell them to stop—not because I want to ruin their fun, but because I don't want them to get hurt.
- What we give up is nothing compared to what we receive. The cost of not becoming a Christian is far greater than the cost of becoming a Christian.
- What we give up is nothing compared to what Jesus gave up for us when He died on the cross for us.

c) "There must be a catch"

Sometimes, people find it hard to accept that there is anything that is free in this life. They think it all sounds too easy. Therefore, they think there must be some hidden trap or catch. However, what they fail to realize is that, although it is free for us, it was not free for Jesus. He paid dearly for it with His own blood. It is easy for us. But it was not easy for Him.

d) "I'm not good enough"

None of us is good enough. Nor can we ever make ourselves good enough for God. But that is why Jesus came. He made it possible for God to accept us just as we are, whatever we have done, and however much of a mess we have made of our lives.

e) "I could never keep it up"

We are right to think we could never keep it up— we cannot, by ourselves. But the Spirit of God, who comes to live within us, gives us the power and the strength to keep going as Christians.

f) "I'll do it later"

This is perhaps the most common excuse. Sometimes people say, " I know it's true—but I am not ready." They put it off. The longer we put it off, the harder it becomes and the more we miss out. We never know whether or not we will get another opportunity. Speaking for myself, my only regret is that I did not accept the gift earlier.

What Do We Have to Do?

The New Testament makes it clear that we have to do something to accept the gift that God offers. This is an act of faith. The disciple John writes, "God so loved the world that he gave his one and only Son, that whoever believes in him shall not perish but have eternal life" (John 3:16). Believing involves an act of faith, based on all that we know about Jesus. It is not blind faith. It is putting our trust in a Person. In some ways it is like the step of faith taken by a bride and groom when they say "I will" on their wedding day.

The way people take this step of faith varies enormously, but I want to describe one way in which you can take this step of faith right now. It can be summarized by three very simple words:

a) "Sorry"

You have to ask God to forgive you for all the things you have done wrong and turn from everything that you know is wrong in your life. This is what the Bible means by "repentance."

b) "Thank you"

You believe that Jesus died for you on the cross.

You need to thank Him for dying for you and for the offer of His free gifts of forgiveness, freedom, and His Spirit.

c) "Please"

God never forces His way into our lives. You need to accept His gift and invite Him to come and live within you by His Spirit.

If you would like to have a relationship with God and you are ready to say these three things, then following is a very simple prayer you can pray that will be the start of that relationship:

Lord Jesus Christ,

I am sorry for the things I have done wrong in my life. (Take a few moments to ask His forgiveness for anything particular that is on your conscience.) Please forgive me. I now turn from everything that I know is wrong.

Thank You that You died on the cross for me so that I could be forgiven and set free.

Thank You that You offer me forgiveness and the gift of Your Spirit. I now receive that gift.

Please come into my life by Your Holy Spirit, to be with me forever.

Thank you, Lord Jesus. Amen.

What Now?

1. Tell Someone

It is important to tell someone in order to underline the decision you have made. Often it is only when you tell someone else that it becomes a reality to you. It is probably best to start by telling someone who you think will be pleased to hear the news!

2. Read the Bible

Once we have received Jesus and put our trust in Him, we become children of God (John 1:12). He is our heavenly Father. Like any father, He wants us to have a close relationship with Him. We develop this relationship as we listen to Him (primarily through the Bible) and as we speak to Him in prayer.

The Bible is the Word of God, and you might find it helpful to begin by reading a few verses of John's Gospel (the fourth book of the New Testament) every day. Ask God to speak to you as you read.

3. Start to speak to God each day (i.e. pray)

Start to speak to God each day in prayer. The following guidelines may be helpful:

A - Adoration
   Praising God for who He is and what He has done.

C - Confession
   Asking God's forgiveness for anything that we have done wrong.

T - Thanksgiving
   Thanking God for health, family, friends, and so on.

S - Supplication
   Praying for ourselves, for our friends, and for others.

4. Join a Lively Church

Church is essentially a gathering of Christians who get together to worship God, to hear what God is saying to them, to encourage one another, and to make friends. It should be a very exciting place to be! I first prayed a prayer like the one on page 22 on February 16, 1974. It changed my life. It is the best and most important thing I have ever done. I trust it will be the same for you!

If you have questions about what you have read please go to our website alphausa.org or alphacanada.org.

Go Deeper

Bible in One Year is a free daily Bible reading resource with commentary by Nicky and Pippa Gumbel. Each day a passage from the Old Testament, a Psalm or Proverb, and a passage from the New Testament are covered so in the course of one year, the whole Bible is read.

Intended to be read or listened to alongside the Bible to provide fresh understanding of the texts, it is available via email, with the Bible in One Year app, and online at bibleinoneyear.org.

The following pages are selected excerpts from Bible in One Year around the theme of Christmas.

bibleinoneyear.org

Merry Christmas

On December 25, we celebrate the "central event in the history of the earth, the very thing the whole story has been about" (C. S. Lewis).[1] We celebrate the birth of Jesus. It is a day of great joy and celebration around the world.

And yet, in the midst of all the trappings and celebrations of Christmas, it can be easy to miss why Jesus' birth is so significant. The key to Christmas lies, not in the details of the shepherds' visit or the wise men's journey, but in the identity of the one whom they came to worship. In Jesus, God became "flesh" and "made his dwelling among us" (John 1:14).

Our New Testament passage for today helps us to grasp something of the enormity of what that means. In it we are reminded that "baby Jesus" is also the "Lord of lords and King of kings" (Revelation 17:14b). We are given a glimpse of the cosmic struggle between good and evil, as a vast array of powers and authorities line up against God, and yet we are reminded that in the end, it is through the humility and self-sacrifice of "the Lamb" that they are overcome.

On Christmas Day we remember the first extraordinary act of humility in this great cosmic drama, as Jesus puts aside the glories of heaven for a humble stall. As the carol, *Hark! The Herald Angels Sing*, puts it:

Christ, by highest heaven adored;
Christ, the everlasting Lord;
late in time behold him come,
offspring of a virgin's womb.
Veiled in flesh the Godhead see;
hail the incarnate Deity,
pleased as man with man to dwell,
Jesus, our Emmanuel.
Hark! The herald angels sing,
'Glory to the new born King!'

In each of today's passages we see the blessings of following this "new born King."

Psalm 147:12–20
1. Blessing, peace and satisfaction
All the promises of God were fulfilled when Jesus came. God promised his people blessing, peace and satisfaction ("the best bread on your tables", v. 14, MSG). He "launches his promises earthward" (v. 15, MSG).

When the birth of Jesus was announced to the shepherds, the angel described it as "good news of great joy for all the people" (Luke 2:10). The heavenly hosts praise God for "peace on earth" (v. 14). Jesus had been born in Bethlehem (meaning "the house of bread"). He is the one who satisfies the spiritual hunger in the heart of every human being. Lord, thank you for the way in which you bless your people.

Thank you that you give us peace—that "we have peace with God through our Lord Jesus Christ" (Romans 5:1). Thank you that you satisfy the deepest longings of our hearts.

New Testament
Revelation 17:1-18
2. Called, chosen and faithful

Christmas is not only a nice story, but a decisive moment in human history. In the cosmic battle between good and evil, God and the devil, Jesus is the decisive figure. That battle, and Jesus' centrality and victory in it, is the focus of our New Testament passage for today.

Sometimes, the church appears to be fighting a losing battle. In Western Europe today, church attendance has been in decline for some time. Secularism appears to be beginning to win. The book of Revelation reveals what is happening behind the scenes, and how things will ultimately turn out.

As we look around at our world, it is immensely powerful, attractive and seductive at one level. Yet, beneath the surface we see so much evil and so much opposition to the Lamb.

The opposition to Jesus is personified in "Babylon the Great, the mother of prostitutes and of the abominations of the earth" (v. 5), which is written on the woman who rides on a beast.

In the original context, the identity of "Babylon" is ancient Rome. As we have seen, the "seven hills on which the woman sits" (v. 9) are the seven hills around Rome.

Superficially, there was something very attractive about the Roman Empire, representing all that the world offers. She is "dressed in purple and scarlet, and was glittering with gold, precious stones and pearls" (v. 4).

But beneath the superficial attraction lay violence and vice: "With her the kings of the earth committed adultery and the inhabitants of the earth were intoxicated with the wine of her adulteries" (v. 2).

It gradually becomes apparent that despite appearances to the contrary, this violence and vice was not random, but specifically targeted against God and his people. The array of characters that appear in the first half of the passage "have one purpose... they will make war against the Lamb" (vv. 13–14).

The wonderful news of this passage is that the Lamb wins. He doesn't only win, but he also includes you in his victory: "They will make war against the Lamb, but the Lamb will overcome them because he is Lord of lords and King of kings – and with him will be his *called, chosen* and *faithful followers*" (v. 14). As the church often comes under great attack and the forces of secularism sometimes seem to be in the ascendancy, I find this verse to be a great comfort and encouragement.

As Mother Teresa said, "God does not call me to be successful; he calls me to be *faithful*." If you are faithful to Jesus you will ultimately be successful, because Jesus will ultimately succeed.

Celebrate today the privilege of being one of those *called*, *chosen* and *faithful* followers of Jesus.

Jesus, the baby, born that first Christmas day, grew up, died as the Lamb of God and was raised to life.

Ultimately the Lamb will overcome because he is Lord of lords and King of kings. That is wonderful news to celebrate this Christmas. As one of the great Christian carols puts it, we have a savior "to free all those who trust in Him from Satan's power and might. O tidings of comfort and joy!"

Lord, thank you that you are Lord of lords and King of kings. Thank you that you rule and reign. Thank you that ultimately the Lamb will overcome all the forces of evil. Help me to stick close to Jesus and be among his faithful followers.

Old Testament
Nehemiah 3:1–4:23
3. Rebuilding, restoring and repairing
Christmas Day especially is a day when, all over the world, the name of Jesus should be honored. Sadly, it is so often not the case. What can we

contribute to seeing the name of Jesus honored in our world?

Jerusalem was the city of God where God dwelt. God had called Nehemiah and the people to rebuild the walls of Jerusalem. This is a wonderful visual illustration of the task of the church today. We are called to rebuild and repair so that the name of Jesus may be honored again in our society.

Do you ever wonder "Am I needed?"; "Do I have anything to offer?"; "Is what I do of any value or significance?"

In this passage we see that everyone was needed. Everyone went to work shoulder to shoulder, side by side, rebuilding, restoring and repairing. Each was given a portion of different lengths. The key is not to compare, but simply to get on with whatever God calls you to do.

God notices what you do and values what you do. 2,500 years later, we are still reading what the people of God did here. Their names are listed.

They were all volunteers. None of them appear to have been professional builders by trade. They were business people, entrepreneurs, rulers, nobles, goldsmiths and perfume-makers. Yet they were willing to offer themselves for the task of rebuilding. All ages were involved (3:12).

They might have been tempted to think that what they were doing did not seem very significant. Malkijah the ruler was asked to repair the Dung Gate! He did not complain that it was beneath him. He simply got on with it. Together they were part of something very significant. They were rebuilding Jerusalem. They were bringing honor to God's name.

Opposition and ridicule came from the outside (4:1–8) and discouragement from within (vv. 10,12). The same was true for Jesus. His birth was not welcomed by all. Herod tried to kill him. The opposition to Jesus and his church continues today. But through a combination of prayer and action, success is possible. When opposition comes, respond like Nehemiah (v. 9). As Joyce Meyer puts it, "Intensify your prayers and increase your vigilance."[2] They never dropped their guard (v. 23).

The key: "Our God will fight for us!" (v.10). With God fighting for us, a nation can be changed, churches can be filled, family life strengthened, marriage honored, the crime rate can fall and society can be transformed. Most important of all, the name of Jesus can be honored again.

As you look around at the state of the church, get involved in this task of rebuilding. Be willing to work hard and not to be put off by opposition.

Lord, thank you that the Lamb always wins— that the one whose birth we celebrate today will ultimately be victorious because he is "King of kings and Lord of lords."

Pippa Adds
Psalm 147:14

"He grants peace…" Or, as it says in Isaiah, "He will be called Wonderful Counselor, Mighty God, Everlasting Father, Prince of Peace. Of the increase of his government and peace there will be no end" (Isaiah 9:6–7a). That's what is needed this Christmas.

Notes:

1. C. S. Lewis, Joyful Christian, (MacMillan Publishing Company, 1984) p.53
2. Joyce Meyer, Everyday Life Bible, (Faithwords, 2013) p.732

Your Key to Life

- Madonna said, "When I was growing up... Jesus Christ was like a movie star, my favorite idol of all."

- Napoleon Bonaparte said, "I know men and I tell you that Jesus Christ is no mere man."

- Novelist H. G. Wells said, "I am an historian, I am not a believer. But this penniless preacher from Galilee is irresistibly the center of history."

Even people who would not describe themselves as followers of the "penniless preacher" recognize that there is something extraordinary about Jesus.

The key to life is Jesus. The key to understanding the Bible is Jesus. The key to understanding God's character is Jesus. The key to getting our lives sorted out is Jesus. No one, not even angels, can compare to Jesus (Hebrews 1:1–14).

If you want to know what God is like, look at Jesus. He said, "Anyone who has seen me has seen the Father" (John 14:9). Everything you read and understand about God through the Bible needs to be read through the lens of Jesus. He is the ultimate revelation of God.

Psalm 119:129–136

1. Jesus provides cleansing from our sins

Reading the Bible is, in some ways, like looking in a mirror with a very bright light: "The unfolding of your words gives light" (v. 130a). The light reveals what is wrong with our lives and what we need to have cleaned up. It reveals the things that cause a barrier between us and God.

This barrier was removed when Jesus provided cleansing for your sins. Through Jesus, you can be confident that God's face will shine upon you (v. 135).

Pray like the psalmist, "Turn to me and have mercy on me, as you always do to those who love your name. Direct my footsteps according to your word; let no sin rule over me. Redeem me from human oppression, that I may obey your precepts. Make your face shine upon your servant" (vv. 132–135a).

The psalmist's prayer foreshadows the great act of Jesus in providing purification for sins. Through Jesus you can always turn to God with confidence knowing that he will have mercy on you, "as [he] always [does] to those who love [his] name" (v. 132).

Lord, thank you for Jesus. Thank you for your mercy. May no sin rule over me. Keep me from pride, anger, lust, greed, envy, prayerlessness, rivalry and all the other temptations of life. I pray that you would make your face shine upon me today.

New Testament
Hebrews 1:1-14
2. Jesus is superior to angels

Jesus is unique and he is all you need. As Eugene Peterson points out, you do not need Jesus-and-angels. You do not need Jesus-and-Moses. You do not need Jesus-and-priesthood. "This letter deletes the hyphens, the add-ons." All you need is Jesus.

The book of Hebrews is all about who Jesus is, and how he is better and greater than any other being, teaching, or religious system. It opens with a comparison between Jesus and the Old Testament prophets. It explains the wonderful truth of how God spoke through the prophets, but then describes how Jesus is even better (vv. 1–3).

He is "the heir of all things", he was involved in creation, he is the ultimate revelation of God, he is your sustainer, and he is your redeemer. The reason for all of this lies in who Jesus is.

Jesus "is the radiance of God's glory and the exact representation of his being" (v. 3). As *The Message* puts it, he "perfectly mirrors God, and is stamped with God's nature."

Jesus came to sort out our lives. "After he had provided purification for sins, he sat down at the right hand of the Majesty in heaven" (v. 3b). Sitting down symbolizes the fact that his work was finished (see also John 19:30).

There have always been people who can't

accept this truth. Today, some argue that Jesus was "just a great religious teacher", and nothing more. In a similar way, at the time of this letter, some people were arguing that Jesus was "just an angel". The writer of Hebrews says: "So he became as much superior to the angels as the name he has inherited is superior to theirs" (Hebrews 1:4). He then goes on to argue the superiority of Jesus over the angels.

There are nearly 300 references to angels in the Bible. What do we know about them?

In this passage we see that angels worship and serve God (vv. 6–7). They are God's messengers (v. 7, MSG). They are spiritual beings who serve Christians (v. 14). They "are sent to serve those who will inherit salvation" (v. 14).

Angels guard and protect you (Psalm 91:11). For example, an angel strengthened Jesus at Gethsemane (Luke 22:43). Each church has one (Revelation chapters 1–3).

But God is *not* their Father (Hebrews 1:5). In this way, Jesus is far superior and every Christian is better off than the angels because God *is* our Father. The writer of Hebrews sets out seven passages from Old Testament scriptures to show the superiority of Jesus over the angels (Psalm 2:7; 2 Samuel 7:14; Deuteronomy 32:43; Psalms 45:6–7; 102:25–27; 104:4; 110:1).

All these passages are the answer to anyone who says that Jesus was only an angel or (more likely today) a "great religious teacher.'" The peak of the argument is in Hebrews 1:8, "About the Son he says, 'Your throne, O God…'"This is an outright ascription of divinity to Jesus.

Lord, thank you that you send angels to guard and protect us. Thank you that they serve us. But thank you even more for Jesus, who is far superior to all angels.

Old Testament
Lamentations 3:40–5:22
3. Jesus is the anointed Messiah

The writer of Lamentations says, "Let us lift up our hearts and our hands" (3:41). The lifting of hearts and hands seem to go together in prayer. Raising hands in prayer is not eccentric or weird, it is the traditional form of prayer in both the Old Testament and New Testament. The writer calls the people to pray and says, "Let's take a good look at the way we're living and reorder our lives under God" (v. 40, MSG). This is an important discipline in a life of faith. Ask God to reveal if there are any areas of your life that you need to change. If there are, then return to God in confession and repentance (v. 42 onwards). Now you know that you will be forgiven and your relationship with God will be restored because of what Jesus has done for you. This passage, like so many others in the Old Testament, points forward to Jesus.

The writer of Lamentations says, "You, O Lord, reign forever; your throne endures from generation to generation" (5:19).

The writer of Hebrews says of Jesus: "'Your throne, O God, will last forever… therefore God, your God, has set you above your companions by anointing you with the oil of joy'" (Hebrews 1:8–9). Jesus is God's anointed one – the Christ, the Messiah.

He is the one to whom all the Scriptures point. The people of God were expecting the Lord's anointed. The writer of Lamentations speaks of 'the Lord's anointed' (Lamentations 4:20). The Hebrew word for anointed one is "Meshiach" from which we get the word Messiah. He goes on to say, "to you also the cup will be passed" (v. 21). Jesus spoke of the cup he would drink (Mark 10:38; John 18:11). Jesus is thinking of the cup of God's wrath against sin.

God's anger is not like ours. It contains no element of spite, pettiness or hypocrisy. It is the reaction of a holy and loving God towards sin. Passages like this help us to understand how serious our sin is in God's sight and how amazing it is that, on the cross, Jesus bore the wrath of God for you and me.

The prophet sees that they are cut off from God by their sin: "You have covered yourself with a cloud so that no prayer can get through" (Lamentations 3:44). This is the barrier that Jesus removed when he drank the cup of God's wrath and provided purification for sins. This is the answer to the prayer of the writer of Lamentations when he prayed, "Restore us to yourself, O Lord, that we may return; renew our days as of old" (5:21).

Because of Jesus, the Anointed One and the one who drank the cup, God's presence is no longer covered with a cloud, and your prayers can get through to him. You can lift up your heart and your hands to God. He will restore you and renew you. Although there are many words about judgment in the Bible, they can be read through the lens of Jesus who revealed the true character of God and provided purification for your sins.

Father, thank you for Jesus. Thank you that the key to life is in Jesus. Thank you that I can know and understand who you are through Jesus.

Pippa Adds
Hebrews 1:7,14
"In speaking of the angels he says, 'He makes his angels winds, his servants flames of fire'"
(v. 7). "Are not all angels ministering spirits sent to serve those who will inherit salvation?"
(v. 14). It is exciting to think there are angels flying around the world bringing help to the people of God.

Notes:

Madonna, SPIN, May 1985.

Bible In One Year

Start your day with the Bible in One Year, a free Bible reading app with commentary by Nicky and Pippa Gumbel. Nicky Gumbel is the Vicar of HTB in London and pioneer of Alpha.

 Now with **NEW** audio commentary

Free to download

 Download on the **App Store**   GET IT ON **Google Play**

Follow us

No smartphone?

Subscribe at bibleinoneyear.org